101
WRITING
PROMPTS
for science fiction writers

MIKE EIMAN

Contents

About The Author   **124**

Beating Writer's Block

It's a fact of life. Whether you're a beginner or a veteran with piles of prose to your name, you will eventually face the terror of a blank page.

Ray Bradbury, best known for books like *Fahrenheit 451*, *The Martian Chronicles* and *The Illustrated Man*, used to describe writer's block as your subconscious warning you that you're doing something wrong. Maybe you're being too political or socially aware. You're writing things to benefit the world, even if you don't truly care about that kind of writing.

"I don't write things to benefit the world," Bradbury once said. "If it happens that they do, swell. I didn't set out to do that. I set out to have a hell of a lot of fun."

So what do you do when your subconscious digs its heels into the ground in the middle of a writing project? A lot of writers become self destructive; they drink alcohol, use drugs and wallow in despair. Negative behavior isn't very useful for beating writer's block. It might make you feel better temporarily, but it never works out in the long run.

A better approach is to take a step back from whatever you're writing. Get to the root cause of whatever is causing the block. Maybe you're overthinking. Maybe you're underthinking. Or maybe you're not being true to yourself.

You're trying to write a dystopian political story because you admire George Orwell, even though you prefer stories about rocket ships and laser guns. You're trying to write a thriller because thrillers make the bestseller lists, despite the fact your inner child is obsessed with time-travelling robots.

That's where a book like this can help. It allows you to choose from more than 100 writing prompts, each giving you a scenario within specific area of science fiction: Aliens, time travel, space travel, robots and more.

The prompts in this book use the pronoun "you," but you can write from any point of view. If you have a character you're trying to develop, drop them into one of these situations and see how they respond. Otherwise, just pretend you're the main character. Trying to make up a new character for each prompt may provide more of a challenge, but it may also cause you to stall.

Give yourself as few excuses as possible to avoid starting. You can shoot for a word count or set a timer. Or you can just write until you don't feel like writing anymore. Don't strain. Don't stress. The main objective, according to Bradbury, is to have a hell of a lot of fun.

What Is Science Fiction?

A book that focuses on science fiction writing must discuss what we mean by "science fiction."

Science fiction is not simply a story involving space, aliens, time travel or any of the other tropes of the genre. But if you want to write about those sorts of things, science fiction is a fine place to put them.

It's possible to write literary fiction involving robots. After all, robots dominate in many areas of the real world. They build cars, manage shipping warehouse and even assist soldiers and police officers in situations too dangerous for humans. A story involving robots is not automatically science fiction.

A time travel story could become an epic fantasy if the characters travel to a time and place with dragons, magic spells and enchanted swords. Or a Western if the time machine takes us to the Old West.

There are many ways to define science fiction. Since it has "science" right there in the name, we're going to think about it scientifically.

The scientific method of writing

The scientific method is the way scientists acquire new knowledge and build on our understanding of how things work.

- Ask questions
- Form a hypothesis
- Make predictions
- Conduct experiments

STEP ONE: Ask questions

Scientific questions can be based on observations (Why does the sun rise in the east and set in the west?), or a desired outcome (How can humans prevent a global nuclear war?)

Great science fiction asks great questions and offers some type of answer. That doesn't mean it's necessarily the right answer. The important part is to look at what's happening today and imagining the consequences in the future.

If you notice people in your everyday life becoming increasingly reliant on mobile phones for everyday interaction, you might ask a question like: What would happen if humans ONLY communicated using electronic devices?

Any time you're having trouble generating ideas for stories, sit down and make a list of questions. You might be surprised how many great ideas jump out at you.

STEP TWO: Form a hypothesis

There's a good chance that any question you ask already has some answers. All you have to do is look for them. The existing answers might be unsatisfactory or seem suspicious. These are the questions that make the best stories.

If you want to write a story about a society that has replaced all in-person communications with text messaging, look for existing theories about the social and psychological effects of electronic communication. Maybe there's a scientific study that goes against your beliefs on the subject.

A simpler example involves answering a question like: Why does the sun rise in the east and set in the west? The science is pretty definitive on this subject. The sun rises in the east because of the way the earth rotates on its axis.

Based on the information you find, you can develop a hypothesis.

STEP THREE: Make predictions

What are the logical consequences of your hypothesis?

Imagine if you wanted to write a story about a world where the earth's rotation was reversed. One likely implication would be the sun rising in the west and setting in the east. What would this do to insects and animals that depend on the sun for navigation? Would this mean clocks would need to run backwards?

STEP FOUR: Conduct experiments

Once you've made some predictions, it's time to test the validity of your hypothesis. How can you test your findings?

Drop some characters into the situation and see what happens. You might find that life is very different in a world where the sun rises and sets in reverse. Or it might make so little difference that it's not even worth writing a full story about.

The Prompts

Now that you have a scientific framework for approaching science fiction, it's time to put that knowledge to the test.

Writing prompts are a great way to sharpen your skills and get your creative juices flowing. There is no formula for writing a great story other than writing a lot, reading a lot and striving to constantly improve your writing. The first time you go through this book, you may only find one or two prompts that inspire you. But a little inspiration is worth far more than the cost of a book.

The next time you find yourself blocked, you might find one or two more prompts that get your gears turning again. That's a huge success.

And the best part is that you can use the same prompt multiple times and get a completely different result. You might choose to free associate, use the scientific method outlined in the previous chapter or use some other approach.

Anything that gets you unstuck and inspires you to face the blank page with joy is a major breakthrough.

The prompts in this book are divided into 10 topics:

- Aliens & UFOs
- Time Travel
- Other Worlds
- Space Travel
- Robots
- Alternate History
- Computers and Artificial Intelligence
- Dystopias
- Clones and Mutants
- Biohacking

Don't feel like you have to start and the beginning and work through to the end. Jump around. Be adventurous. Push yourself to write in a sub-genre that you're not totally comfortable with.

But whatever you do, have fun doing it.

ALIENS & UFOS

Take me to your leader

Aliens have just invaded Earth. They threaten to blow up the planet unless you take them to your leader. You don't exactly have the President on speed dial, so you'll need to improvise. What do you do?

2.

Deep-fried Flarg tentacles

You buy lunch at an alien deli. The meal is tasty despite some odd ingredients (mmm, deep-fried flarg tentacles). You start to feel weird but not necessarily sick. What happens next?

3.

Disgruntled alien

You're driving to work when an alien beams down into the passenger seat. It seems to be drunk and complaining about its job. Write about the ensuing conversation. What is the alien's job? Are you scared or excited about meeting a real-life alien?

4.

Decisions, decisions

It's pouring rain, so you're stuck indoors watching TV for the night. Suddenly, reruns of your favorite show are interrupted by an extraterrestrial signal. Through the static, you can hear a couple of bored alien officials debating whether they should abduct you or simply erase your brain. They seem to be aware of your every move, but not of the fact that you can hear them. What happens next?

5.

Alien salesman

Late one night, the Mother Ship beckons you out to the front porch where it captures you with its tractor beam. Rather than probing you, the aliens try to sell you insurance, cutlery or something else you don't want. How do you handle the situation?

6.

A bright light

You're the sheriff of a small rural community. Several residents have been to your office today to report aliens abducted them during the night. You don't believe any of it until you see a bright light outside your window. What's outside?

7.

Leave my cows alone

Someone keeps coming to your farm to mutilate cattle and make crop circles in your fields. You suspect the kids from a neighboring farm are responsible, until one day you find evidence that points to something from another world. What is it? What does it mean?

8.

Canteen, snacks & a knife

A meteor crashes in the woods. You just happen to be hiking nearby and decide to investigate. The meteor is actually a flying saucer. The hatch opens to reveal a terrifying extraterrestrial creature.

All you have with you is a canteen, some snacks and a Swiss Army knife. What do you do?

9.

Get outta my house

It's 3 a.m. and your dog is barking like crazy. You make your way to the kitchen to find a creature with a big head and black eyes making a pot of coffee. Despite your attempts to yell at the creature and threaten it with nearby weapons, it doesn't seem to acknowledge your presence. How do you get the creature out of your home?

10.

Out of gas

While you and some friends drive through the desert to Las Vegas, you notice a strange light in the night sky. It gets brighter and brighter. Suddenly, your car runs out of gas even though you had a half-tank moments earlier. What happens next?

TIME TRAVEL

11.

But I'm from the future!

You travel back in time to warn yourself about an impending disaster. What is the disaster, and how do you make your younger self believe what you're saying?

12.

A terrible crime

A police officer from the future knocks on your door and tells you your best friend is about to commit a terrible crime. He needs your help to prevent the crime and bring your friend to justice. In order to ensure your compliance, the officer injects you with a poison that will kill you unless he gives you the antidote within 24 hours.

What crime is your friend supposed to commit? How do you convince him/her to follow you? Bonus points if you can find a way to get the antidote without handing over your friend.

13.

One hundred years hence

You jump in your time machine and head 100 years into the future. What kind of transportation are people using? What passes for entertainment? What do people eat? Where do they live? Write down anything else you notice.

14.

Drunken brawl with Lincoln

After getting into a drunken brawl with Abraham Lincoln in 1861, you return home to the present day to find that police are waiting for you. Why were you fighting with Honest Abe? What do you tell the police?

15.

Strange relics of a dead world

Your time machine malfunctions and takes you 10,000 years into the future. There is no sign of human life. You find an object in a decaying building that explains where everyone went. What is the object? Where did everybody go?

16.

The lottery dilemma

A friend has discovered a way to travel back in time 20 minutes. It will only work once. You come up with a hairbrained scheme to get the winning lottery numbers, travel back 20 minutes and buy a lotto ticket.

Come up with at least five obstacles that delay or prevent you from buying your ticket before the numbers are announced. What happens?

17.

Cryogenically frozen

After being diagnosed with a terminal illness, you opt to be cryogenically frozen until a cure is found. You awaken 2,000 years in the future. Doctors cure your illness and set you loose (with a hefty hospital bill). Describe how you feel after being unfrozen in the future and your thoughts about missing the past two millennia.

18.

Reflecting on the past

If you could go back in time to change any event in your life, what would it be? Why? Think about how changing the event would affect your current situation.

19.

The backwards-running clock

While waiting in the dentist's office for your 2 p.m. appointment, you notice the clock is running backwards. In fact, time is running backwards! Describe what you see as other patients come and go in reverse. (You might need to make a list to figure out how this would work.)

20.

Time travel with Dr. Wells

It's the year 3500. You arrange a meeting with Dr. Wells, the head time traveler of a university history department. Wells agrees to take you to a particular time period (ancient Egypt, colonial America, 21st century Europe, etc.) that you are researching. Come up with one or more questions about that time period (what was Napoleon's favorite soup?) and describe the answers you find.

> _Note: This doesn't require any actual research. You might decide Napoleon's favorite soup was Campbell's chicken noodle, which he ate from a bucket using a small shovel._

33

OTHER WORLDS

21.

This planet's too hot

You've landed on a planet where the average daily temperature is really freakin' hot. Your job is to make the planet more habitable. Write about some of your ideas to cool things off. This could be a giant pair of sunglasses, a really big refrigerator or anything else that comes to mind.

22.

This planet's too cold

Similar to the last prompt, you've landed on a planet where temperatures are super cold. What are some ways you can make the planet warmer? Describe the process of how you will implement one or more of these ideas. Once again, it can be something silly like a giant bonfire.

23.

This planet just ain't right

You've arrived on a planet where the gravity and atmospheric conditions allow people to fly around like birds. Describe a trip from your home to your favorite store across town. Do you have any near collisions with other flyers?

24.

A shocking adventure

Your spaceship breaks down on a planet that has massive electrical storms every 10 minutes or so. Describe your travels to the nearest human settlement to buy parts for your ship. Think about the potential dangers (i.e. lightning strikes, flooding, ground-shaking thunder).

25.

Bizarre animal planet

You've just landed on a jungle planet teeming with life. Describe some of the the unusual species. Are they friendly? (Tip: Try combining two or more animals you're familiar with.)

26.

Giant slugs

Imagine landing on a planet inhabited by giant slug-like creatures that want to eat you. If you climb to the top of Salt Mountain, you might be able to cause a rockslide that will stop the slugs in their slime trails. Write about the climb and your attempt to evade capture.

27.

An upside-down land

Your spaceship lands on a world very similar to Earth except the gravity flips periodically. One minute you're on the ground, and the next minute you're on the ceiling. Write about your journey up the stairs of a large skyscraper.

28.

Dessert-ed planet

Describe a world made of your favorite dessert. How does it smell? What is it like to walk around on it? Does anybody live there, or do you have free rein to to eat an entire planet?

29.

Moon prison

After insulting the ruler of your home planet, you're banished to a prison colony on the moon. What is a typical day like in moon prison? Describe your cell, fellow inmates, food, etc.

30.

A sign from above

You've crash landed onto a planet of creatures who believe you are a god who has fallen from the sky. How do you handle the situation? What happens if you try to explain that you're not a god?

SPACE TRAVEL

31.

Stranded cargo ship

En route to your home world, you and your crew encounter a cargo ship stranded in space. Standard procedures require you to stop and offer assistance. Who or what is aboard the stranded ship. What happens next?

32.

A sign of life

Your spaceship is floating in orbit while you gather scientific data about an asteroid. The computer finds something strange about the asteroid, possibly signs of life. How do you react to his discovery? What did you find?

33.

Martian vacation

The engines of your commercial space flight fail on the way to a vacation resort on Mars. The captain activates a distress beacon.

A nearby ship stops to assist. Who is it? Are they friend or foe?

34.

Luxury space yacht

You and your family won an all-expenses-paid trip on a luxury space yacht. Describe the sights, sounds, entertainment and anything else you notice during your voyage.

35.

Asteroid field!

As your spaceship hurtles through the cosmos, you and your copilot realize you're closing in on an asteroid field. There's no time to stop or change course before you reach the field. Write about the ordeal. Do you have what it takes to make it out alive?

36.

Trapped with the enemy

While docking with a Sovereign Republic space station to refuel and get fresh supplies, you get a transmission informing your home planet has declared war on the Republic. The airlock opens. Who is on the other side? How do they react to your presence?

37.

Not enough escape pods

You awaken from hypersleep to find that the computer malfunctioned. Instead of sleeping for 50 years, 500 years have passed. Only one of the escape pods still works, meaning only two members of the 20-member crew can escape. How do you decide who lives? How do your crewmates react?

38.

Descent into madness

You're on a 36-year mission to the Crab Nebula when a freak accident causes you to jettison some of your supplies, including the medication that keeps you from going stir crazy. Describe your descent into madness.

39.

Hubble Space conspiracy

While making repairs to the Hubble Space Telescope, you notice the lens cap has been on since the
telescope launched in 1990. Do you try to alert
others to the problem? Or do you keep it to yourself
because there's likely some kind of conspiracy at
play?

40.

Strange activity on the moon

Your space shuttle's computer notices some unusual activity during a routine orbit of the moon. It appears that something is moving on the, presumably, lifeless lunar surface. Upon closer inspection, you're shocked by what the computer has found. What's down there? What does it mean?

ROBOTS

41.

Your own service robot

Your parents just brought home the family's first service robot. It cooks, cleans and even folds your laundry. During a lull in the robot's daily routine, you decide to ask it to do some ridiculous tasks. Come up with three to five tasks and describe how the robot tries to comply.

42.

I swear I'm not human!

Evil robots are marching around town rounding up humans to enslave. You figure out how to evade capture by pretending to be a robot. Describe an interaction with a robot that doesn't quite believe your act.

43.

Machines took your job

You've just learned your job (it can be your actual job or an imaginary one) is being outsourced to robots. Write about the meeting where your boss announces the change and describe how it makes you feel.

44.

Self-driving terror

Imagine a future where the roads are filled with self-driving cars. One day, a glitch causes the machines to seek revenge against their human captors. How do you escape the killer cars and get to safety?

45.

My best friend is a robot

A close friend of yours reveals they are actually a robot. Maybe they even prove it to you by exposing part of their mechanical endoskeleton. How does it make you feel to know your friend is a robot and lied to you about it?

46.

A grumpy vacuum cleaner

The robotic vacuum cleaner you bought is going on strike because you're such a slob. You can't return the vacuum because you're still in the 90-day contract period. How do you deal with this grumpy little robot?

47.

Don't demolish my house!

Your neighbor's old house has been slated for demolition. The autonomous robots doing the work seem to have made a mistake and are headed your way. Describe what obstacles you will place in the robots' paths to keep them from knocking down your house.

48.

Robotic doppelgänger

You come home from a long day at work to find out the robot look-alike you bought to help make you more productive has stolen your family. Your loved ones don't know the difference. How do you confront your family and prove you're the real you?

49.

Nanobots in your blood

A mad scientist has injected a swarm of nanobots into your bloodstream. It will kill you within 12 hours unless you can find a way to extract it. What do you do?

50.

The idea machine

You hire a super-intelligent robot to generate a brilliant idea for new invention that will make you a millionaire. The robot gives you the idea, but threatens to post it on the Internet unless you pay a hefty ransom. Describe the ensuing argument.

ALTERNATE HISTORY

51.

Brontosaurus attack

Dinosaurs never went extinct. Instead, they coexist with primitive humans. Your village is being trampled by a giant brontosaurus. How do you and your tribe deal with this beast using only rocks, spears and other crude tools?

52.

Pay your taxes, peasant!

You are a peasant in a 21st century where armies never advanced beyond medieval knights with armor, swords and horses. One day, a knight shows up at your door to collect unpaid income taxes. You don't have the money. What happens next?

53.

The endless Ice Age

A global Ice Age has lasted well into the present day. Imagine a trip to the grocery store to buy bread. How do you get there? How are you dressed? What technology exists to keep people warm?

54.

A kind of utopia

Following World War II, the Allied powers establish a utopian world government. There is plenty of food, wealth and material goods for everyone. But the system depends on not allowing anyone to live past the age of 30. Tomorrow is your 30th birthday. Imagine a conversation with a close friend or loved one on your final day before execution.

55.

Ashes of industry

The Industrial Revolution failed due to an insufficient supply of coal and oil to keep factories running. Describe a horse ride through an abandoned industrial district. What technology exists without industrialism?

56.

Where has all the oil gone?

A series of bombings decimated most of the world's oil supply almost 20 years ago. Describe the aftermath of living in a former oil town. How has civilization adapted to the lack of oil? Solar power? Increased use of coal? What does transportation look like?

57.

The bombers are coming

Enemy planes have just bombed a city near yours. You know you're next. How do you react? Did you prepare for this day by building a bomb shelter, or are you going to flee with scores of other scared citizens?

58.

From the moon, with love

NASA continued the Apollo program well into the 2000s. Earth has established a research colony on the moon. Describe your feelings after receiving a letter inviting you to spend a month at the lunar colony.

59.

Surviving the flood

A massive global flood has forced humans to occupy large population centers that are as far inland as possible. Describe the cramped living conditions of one of these mega cities.

60.

A world without lightbulbs

The lightbulb was never invented. Describe a familiar room without any artificial light. What would you use instead? Candles? Skylights and windows? Mirrors?

COMPUTERS & ARTIFICIAL INTELLIGENCE

For Science Fiction Writers

61.

The smartest computer

You've been granted access to the smartest computer ever invented. You may ask it only one question. How do you feel about the situation? What do you ask? What answer does the computer give you?

62.

Your identity has been erased

A computer virus has erased your identity, your bank accounts and any record of your existence. Police pull you over for a broken taillight and determine your ID is phony. How are you going to talk your way out of this?

63.

High-tech goes haywire

Your new house uses a sophisticated artificial intelligence system to operate and maintain the electrical system, plumbing, appliances and even keep the yard in top shape. One day, the computer malfunctions and causes everything to go haywire. Write about performing a basic task like doing your laundry or making a sandwich during this ordeal.

64.

You will die tomorrow

You're watching videos on your computer when suddenly the machine begins to talk to you. It says you will die in a terrible accident tomorrow. You press it for more information, but the computer keeps repeating the same few words. Write about how this makes you feel. What do you do?

65.

Complete the mission

While on a leisure drive in your self-driving car, the onboard computer veers off course and starts talking about "the mission." You don't know what it's talking about and beg the car to resume its regular course. Where is it taking you? What is the mission?

66.

Meet your doctor

Following an operation to remove a life-threatening tumor, you ask to thank the doctor who operated on you. Nurses wheel in the AI computer that controlled the robotic instruments. How do you feel knowing a human didn't perform the operation?

67.

Rogue computer

Your computer has gone rogue, sending threatening emails to public officials and hacking into government databases. The FBI shows up and starts asking you about algorithms, nodes and pings. You don't know what they're saying. Then something happens that makes them question your involvement. What happens?

68.

A hypnotic new game

You've just downloaded the new video game everyone's raving about. Before you can try it out, a friend begins playing the game. Your friend becomes hypnotized and can't stop playing. All you can see is a blank screen. How do you help your friend?

69.

VR vacation

A new virtual reality computer system allows you to visit any place in your town without ever leaving home. Where would you go? What would it be like to interact with other people who aren't actually there?

70.

Self-aware cellphone

Your cellphone has become self aware. It's calling everyone you know and leaving obscene messages. The power button doesn't work. Keep in mind that destroying it will leave you with no record of who it called. How do you make it stop?

DYSTOPIAS

71.

Sacrifice to the volcano god

You live in a world where people worship a volcano. They rely on human sacrifice to appease the volcano god so it won't erupt and destroy everything. You or a loved one have been selected to be sacrificed. What do you do?

72.

Please don't take my spoons!

The government owns everything and forces you to rent everyday goods, ranging from silverware to housing. You fell behind on your payments for spoons. Describe a scene between you and a government official who has come to reclaim your spoons.

73.

This child is yours now

You live in a world where children are taken from their parents at birth and assigned to caretakers based on a random career assignment at the age of twelve. For example, a banker would be assigned to parents in the banking industry. Write about a child who shows up at your home to be your apprentice.

74.

Avoiding a shakedown

The ruling class in your society has the legal right to pick you up by your ankles and confiscate any items that fall out. You're carrying your mother's life savings to the bank when you see a Ruler heading your way after shaking down another peasant. How can you make it to the bank without getting robbed?

75.

Sneaking in your sleep

A totalitarian government monitors your every move from the time you wake up until the time you go to sleep. You've begun sneaking out during your assigned sleep time. How do you fool the cameras? How are you enjoying your unlawful freedom?

76.

Join your 'impure' brethren

In a world of strict genetic requirements, those deemed "impure" are gathered onto a boat and sent drifting out to sea. Write about being forced onto one of these boats. What do some of the "impure" people look like? Where do you think the boat will end up?

77.

A fight to the death

There is a shortage of housing. Your friend is chosen to fight another citizen to the death to decide who gets to keep their home. Write about a conversation with your friend about the situation. How do you both feel?

78.

Sent to the dungeon

For the crime of staring at the King, you have been sentenced to spend an afternoon shackled in a dungeon listening to other inmates being tortured. Describe the dungeon (sights, sounds, smells). Talk about the incident and subsequent criminal trial that got you here in the first place.

79.

Life in prison

You were born and raised inside of a prison. A fellow inmate tells you they've found a way out. What does the escape entail? Describe your feelings as you see sunlight and the outside world for the first time.

80.

Painting the Leader

A totalitarian regime forces all workers deemed nonessential to sit around painting portraits of The Leader all day. You are among this group of painters. One day a hand cramp leaves you unable to continue. What are the consequences? Is there any hope of escape?

CLONES AND MUTANTS

81.

The more the merrier

The lab has just completed your order for five clones of yourself. Write about why you wanted the clones in the first place. Imagine explaining your decision to a close friend or loved one.

82.

It wasn't me. It was my clone!

A clone of yourself has just robbed a bank and fled. The police try to arrest you by mistake. Your clone shows up and blames you for the crime. Fortunately, you notice something that ties him/her to the robbery. How do you explain the situation to the police?

83.

Hybrid pet shop

You've just adopted a new pet. It's a cross between two or more of your favorite animals. What does it look like? How does it behave? Is it domesticated?

84.

Half man, half animal

A freak accident has transformed you into a hybrid between a human and your favorite animal. What do you look like? What abilities do you have as a result of your transformation?

85.

Tyrannosaurus domesticus

Scientists have figured out a way to genetically engineer a domesticated tyrannosaurus rex. Write about an average day caring for your new pet.

86.

You're a clone!

A friend or loved one informs you that you are a clone, and the real you died in a car crash five years ago. Write about the conversation and how this revelation makes you feel.

87.

Cloning your pet

After cloning a beloved pet that died long ago, you start to notice it's behavior is a little unusual. It's disappearing every night and returning home covered in blood. Where is your pet going? What's it up to?

88.

Flying mutant children

You're a journalist for a well-regarded science publication. A small town has caught your attention because children are being born there with a mutation that allows them to fly. Describe your observations of parents in this town trying to raise flying children.

89.

Replaced by clones!

Your entire family has been kidnapped and replaced by clones. How do you figure out they're not really your family? How do they react when confronted?

90.

A weird kind of restaurant

A new restaurant has gained national attention for serving unusual meals, including plants and animals that don't exist in nature. Describe your experience dining at the restaurant. What kinds of people are there? What do you order? How does it taste.

BIOHACKING

91.

Robo strength

If you had a robotic exoskeleton that gave you incredible strength (lift cars, demolish buildings, etc.), what would you do with your abilities?

92.

The mindreading serum

You've signed up for trial injections of a drug that allows you to read minds. Where would you go to try it out? What would it be like to interact with people who don't know you can hear their thoughts?

93.

You are immortal

Doctors have given you artificial organs that will last for hundreds of years, meaning you're essentially immortal. How would this affect your outlook on life? Would you be more willing to take risks? Or would you become a shut-in for fear of getting hit by a truck or something?

94.

Erasing the past

Scientists discover a process for erasing childhood memories. Think of a memory, good or bad, and imagine that it was erased. Describe the how losing this memory might change your outlook on things.

95.

No more sleeping

You undergo a procedure to modify your DNA so you don't need to sleep anymore. What would life be like without sleep? What would you do with the extra time?

96.

30 seconds in the future

Your doctor implants a computer in your brain that allows you to accurately predict 30 seconds into the future. Imagine having an important conversation with a loved one or coworker. Describe the experience of knowing what the other person will say before they say it.

97.

Swiss Army hands

You decide to have your hands replaced with robotic hands that contain a wide array of tools. What tools would you request? How would you use them in real life?

98.

The x-ray police officer

You're a police officer who has undergone a new eye surgery that allows you to see through walls. An armed suspect has just taken a woman hostage and is hiding inside of an abandoned building. Describe what you see. How do you save the woman without getting her killed?

99.

Your new wings

The bandages have just come off of your newly grafted wings. You decide to fly around your hometown. What do you see? How do you feel? How are other people reacting?

100.

Running like the wind

A series of injections has given you the ability to run up to 80 miles per hour (about 130 km/h). Write about a crosstown trip from your home or office to a business meeting. Keep in mind that the road is still full of cars, and be mindful of pedestrians.

101.

Choose your superpower

A mad scientist tells you he can hack your DNA to give you any superpower you can imagine. But you can only have one power. What power would you choose? Why? Write about a scenario in which you use your newfound power.

About The Author

Mike Eiman is a lifelong resident of Fresno, CA. He graduated from California State University Fresno in 2010 with a bachelor's degree in theatre arts and a minor in mass communications and journalism.

Mike writes science fiction, as well as articles about the art and business of writing. He worked as a journalist for seven years, primarily covering local governments, law enforcement and criminal justice.

For more about Mike and his other work, visit www.mikeeiman.com.